EASY CLASSIC *Duets*

7 GREAT ARRANGEMENTS

BY GLENDA AUSTIN, ERIC BAUMGARTNER AND CAROLYN MILLER

INCLUDES ONLINE AUDIO

The online audio tracks give you the flexibility to rehearse or perform these piano duets anytime and anywhere. Each piece features a Secondo part, a Primo part, and a demo track of both parts together that can be downloaded or streamed. The **Playback+** feature allows you to change the tempo without altering the pitch!

PLAYBACK+
Speed • Pitch • Balance • Loop

To access audio, visit:
www.halleonard.com/mylibrary

Enter Code
7160-4801-6037-3440

ISBN 978-1-4950-2129-9

WILLIS MUSIC

EXCLUSIVELY DISTRIBUTED BY

HAL•LEONARD®

Visit Hal Leonard Online at
www.halleonard.com

World headquarters, contact:
Hal Leonard
7777 West Bluemound Road
Milwaukee, WI 53213
Email: info@halleonard.com

In Europe, contact:
Hal Leonard Europe Limited
1 Red Place
London, W1K 6PL
Email: info@halleonardeurope.com

In Australia, contact:
Hal Leonard Australia Pty. Ltd.
4 Lentara Court
Cheltenham, Victoria, 3192 Australia
Email: info@halleonard.com.au

ABOUT THE ARRANGERS

Glenda Austin is a composer, arranger, pianist, and teacher from Joplin, Missouri. A graduate of the University of Missouri, Glenda teaches music in elementary and high school, and is an adjunct faculty member at Missouri Southern State University. She is a frequent adjudicator and clinician for Willis and Hal Leonard, presenting piano workshops for teachers and students throughout the United States, as well as in Canada and Japan. Several of Glenda's compositions appear on state repertoire lists, and two best-sellers, "Jazz Suite No. 2" and "Sea Nocturne," are perennial favorites on the National Federation list.

Eric Baumgartner received jazz degrees from Berklee College of Music in Boston and DePaul University in Chicago. He is the author and creator of the *Jazzabilities* and *Jazz Connection* series, a related set of beginning jazz piano books. Besides composing and maintaining a teaching studio, Eric works extensively in musical theatre and plays keyboard and guitar with several pop and jazz groups. He is the orchestrator of several noted Willis publications, including the *Teaching Little Fingers to Play* series, *Popular Piano Solos,* and his own *Jazz It Up!* series. His wide range of musical influences is reflected in his balanced approach to teaching: he finds validity in all music and works with students to help them find their own musical identity through improvising, arranging, and composing. Eric has presented his unique teaching techniques in the United States, England, and Australia.

Carolyn Miller holds a bachelor's degree from the College Conservatory of Music at the University of Cincinnati and a master's degree in elementary education from Xavier University. A lifelong educator, Carolyn has taught piano to students of all ages, privately and in the classroom, and continues to maintain a piano studio in her Cincinnati home. She presents workshops throughout the United States and is often asked to adjudicate at music festivals and competitions. Carolyn's music often teaches essential technical skills, yet is fun to play, making it appealing to children and adults and resulting in frequent appearances on the National Federation list. In fact, well-known personality Regis Philbin performed two of her compositions, "Rolling River" and "Fireflies," live on national television.

CONTENTS

By the Beautiful Blue Danube

SECONDO

Johann Strauss, Jr.
1825–1899
Arranged by Eric Baumgartner

By the Beautiful Blue Danube

PRIMO

Johann Strauss, Jr.
1825–1899
Arranged by Eric Baumgartner

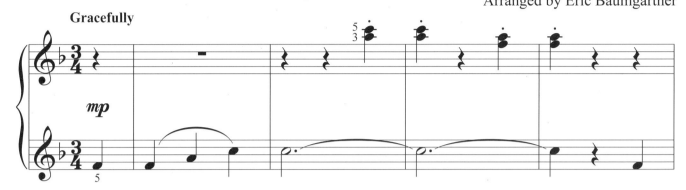

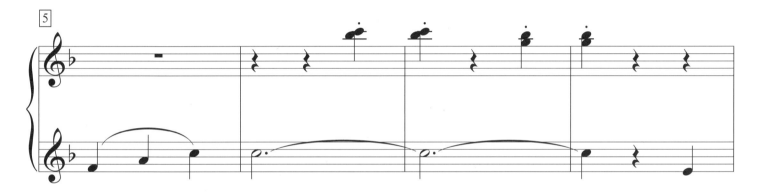

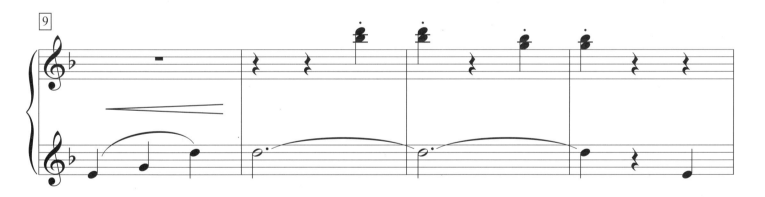

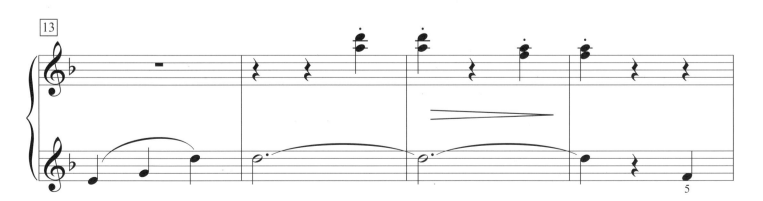

6

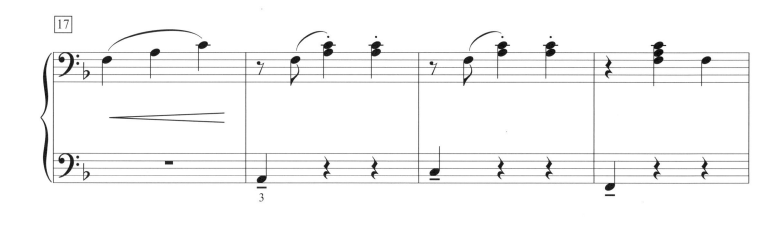

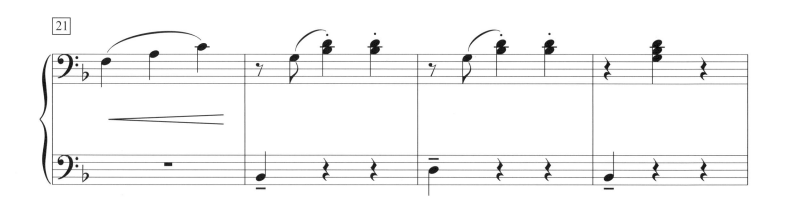

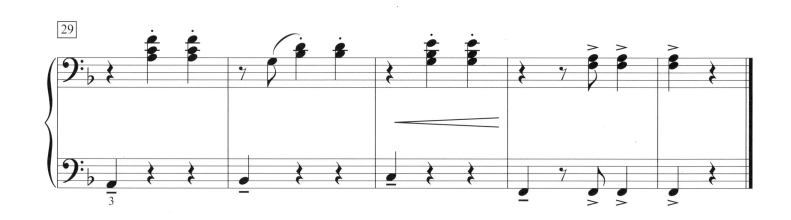

PRIMO

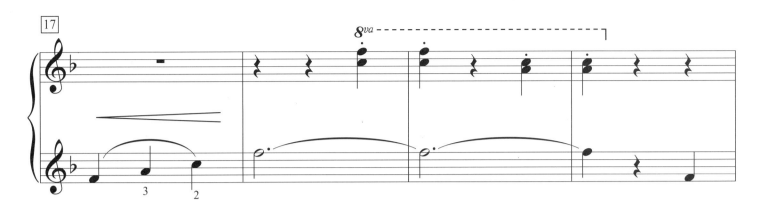

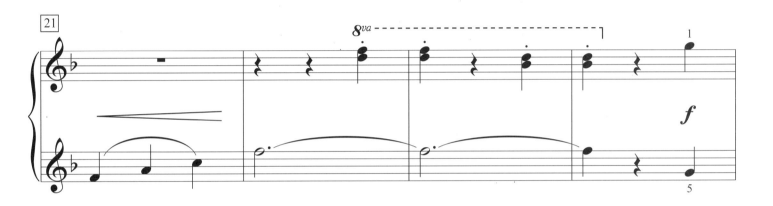

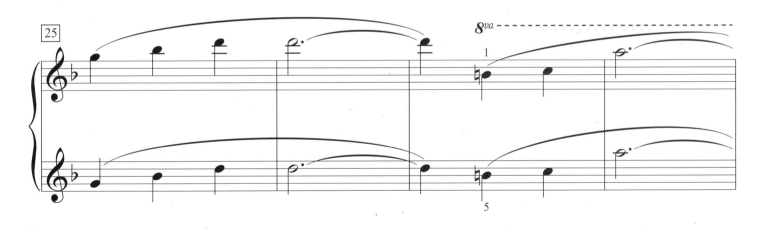

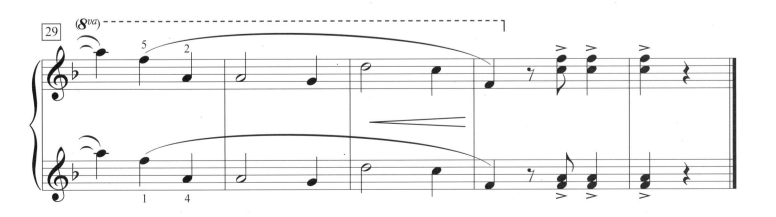

Eine Kleine Nachtmusik
("Serenade")
First Movement Excerpt

SECONDO

Wolfgang Amadeus Mozart
1756–1791
Arranged by Eric Baumgartner

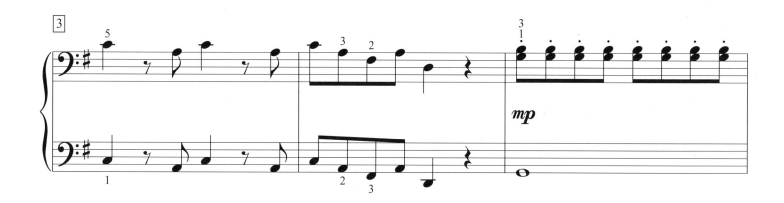

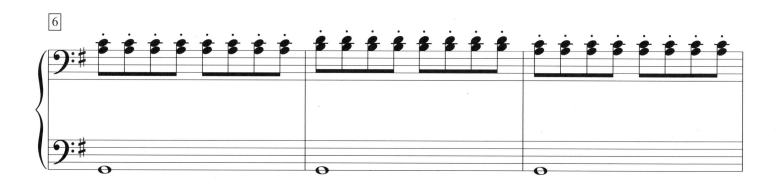

Eine Kleine Nachtmusik
("Serenade")
First Movement Excerpt

PRIMO

Wolfgang Amadeus Mozart
1756–1791
Arranged by Eric Baumgartner

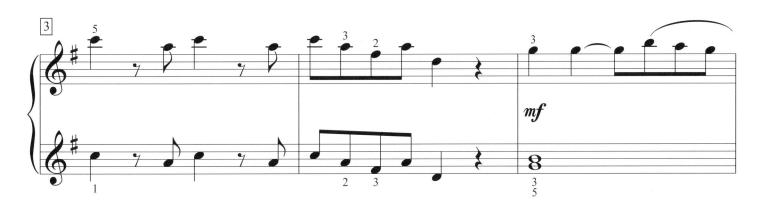

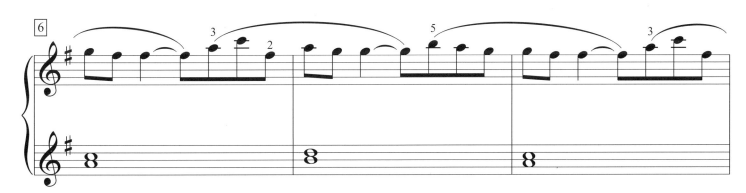

SECONDO

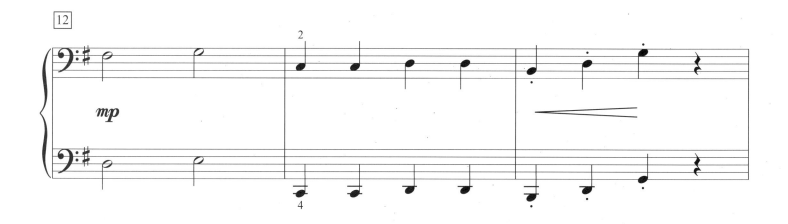

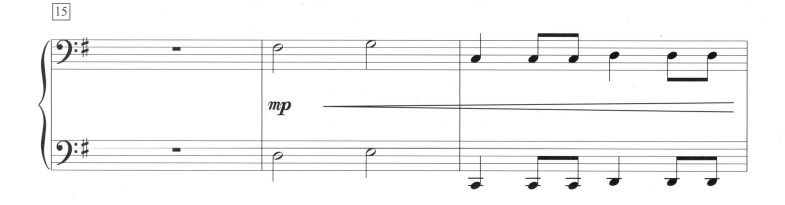

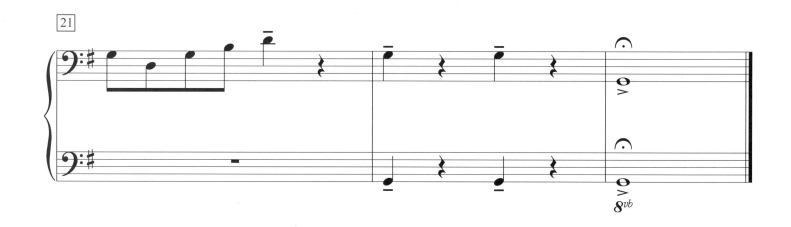

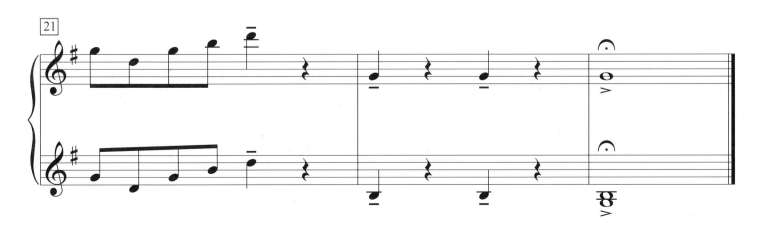

Hungarian Dance No. 5

SECONDO

Johannes Brahms
1833–1897
Arranged by Carolyn Miller

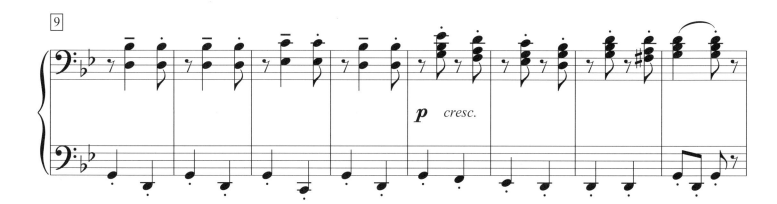

Hungarian Dance No. 5

PRIMO

Johannes Brahms
1833–1897
Arranged by Carolyn Miller

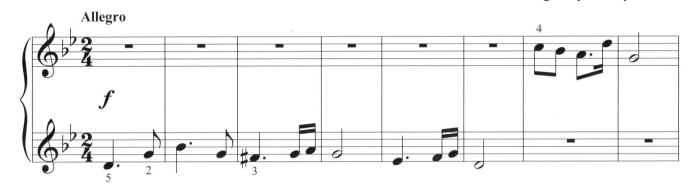

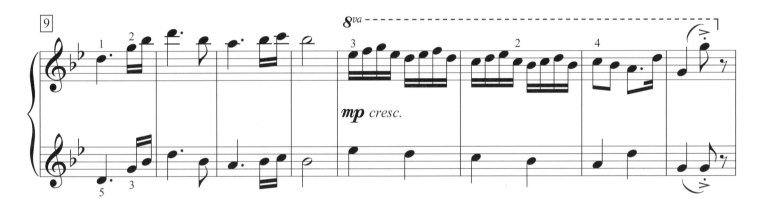

SECONDO

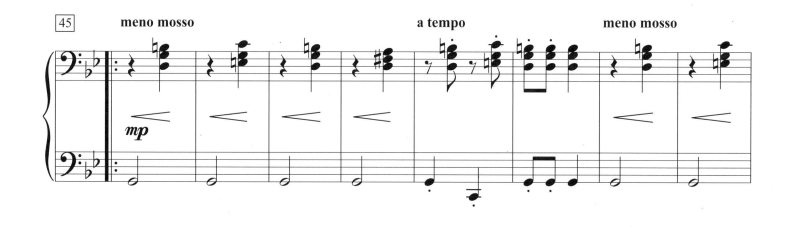

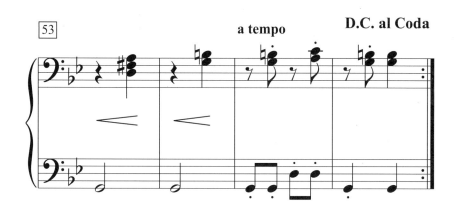

PRIMO

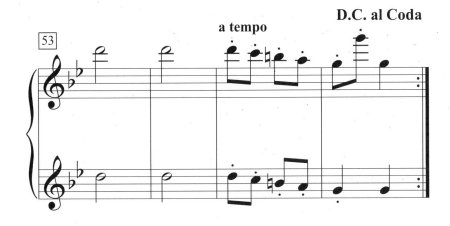

Morning
from PEER GYNT

SECONDO

Edvard Grieg
1843–1907
Arranged by Glenda Austin

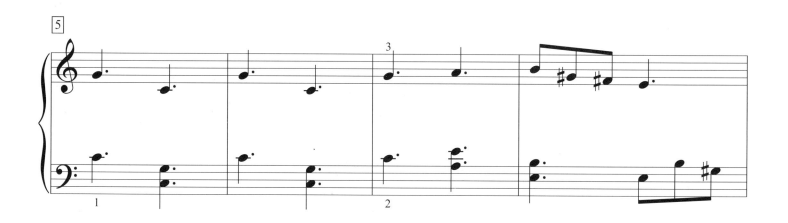

Morning
from PEER GYNT

PRIMO

Edvard Grieg
1843–1907
Arranged by Glenda Austin

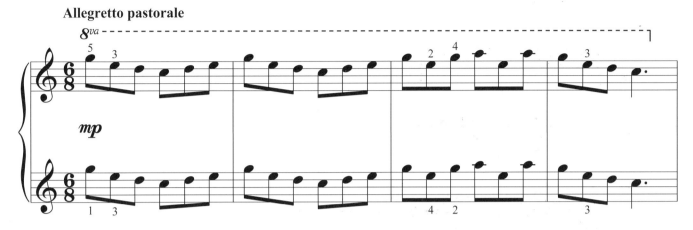

SECONDO

Rondeau

SECONDO

Jean-Joseph Mouret
1682–1738
Arranged by Carolyn Miller

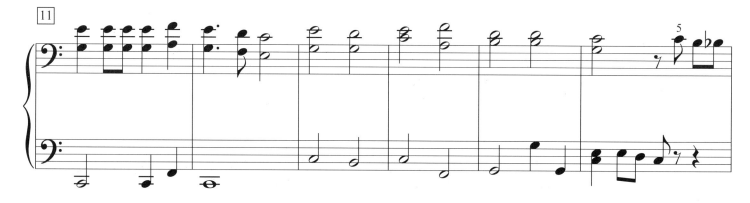

Play quarter notes detached.

Rondeau

PRIMO

Jean-Joseph Mouret
1682–1738
Arranged by Carolyn Miller

Majestically

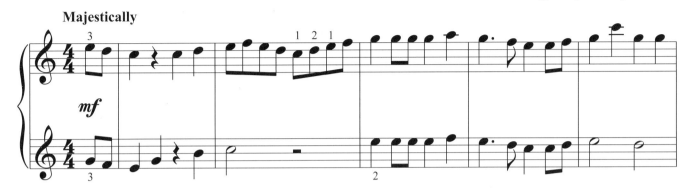

Play quarter notes detached.

SECONDO

PRIMO

The Sleeping Beauty Waltz

SECONDO

Pyotr Il'yich Tchaikovsky
1840–1893
Arranged by Glenda Austin

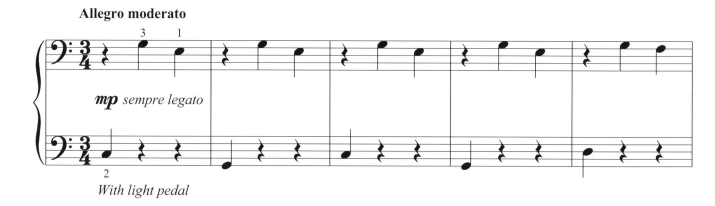

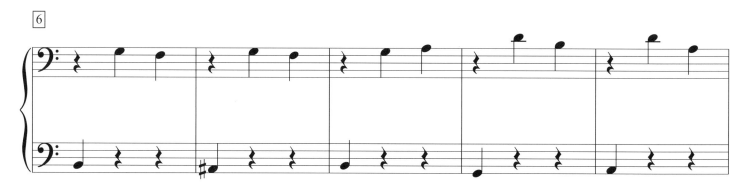

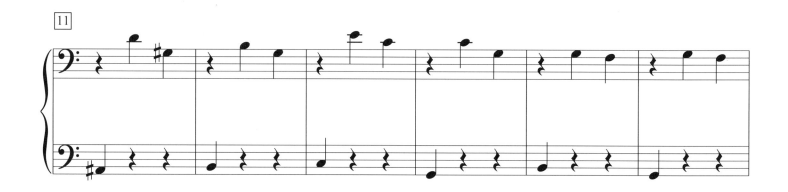

The Sleeping Beauty Waltz

PRIMO

Pyotr Il'yich Tchaikovsky
1840–1893
Arranged by Glenda Austin

SECONDO

PRIMO

Symphony No. 94 in G Major
("Surprise")
Second Movement Excerpt

SECONDO

Franz Joseph Haydn
1732–1809
Arranged by Carolyn Miller

Symphony No. 94 in G Major

("Surprise")
Second Movement Excerpt

PRIMO

Franz Joseph Haydn
1732–1809
Arranged by Carolyn Miller

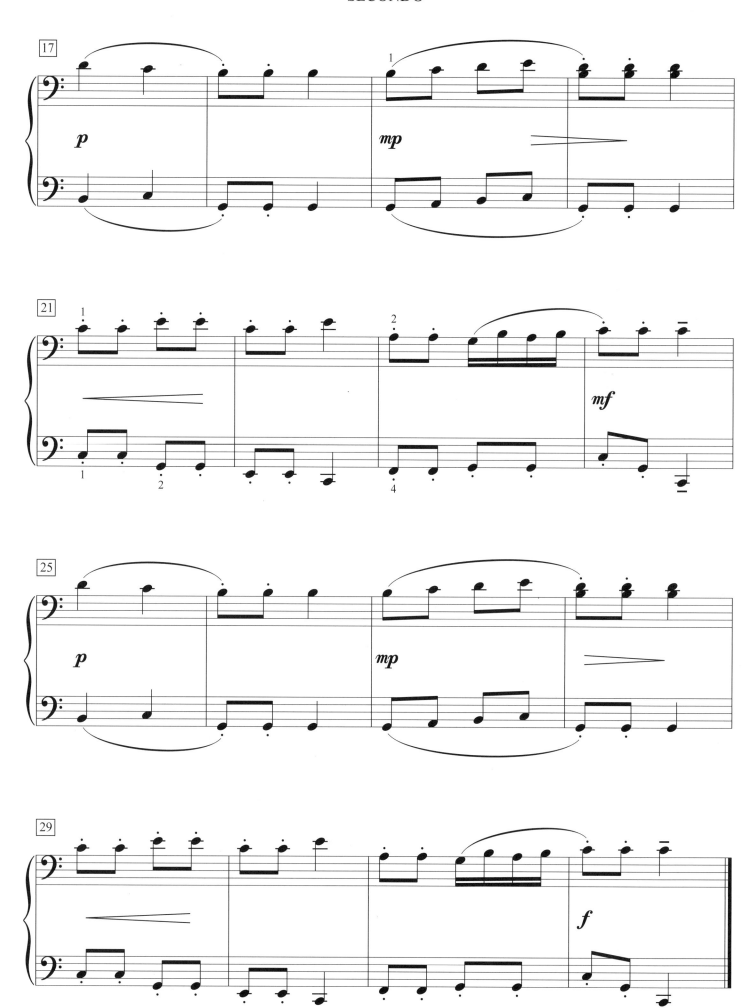

ALSO AVAILABLE

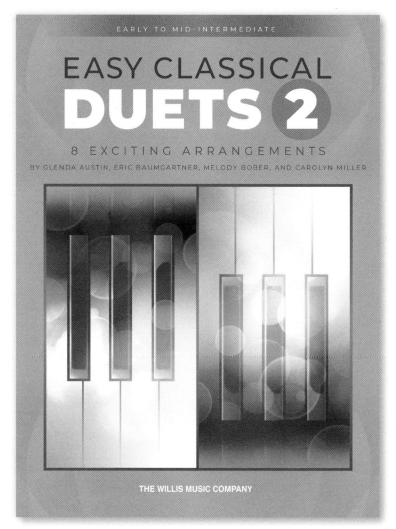

HL00396991

Canon in D | **JOHANN PACHELBEL**, arr. Melody Bober

Flower Duet | **LÉO DELIBES**, arr. Glenda Austin

Jesu, Joy of Men's Desiring | **J. S. BACH**, arr. Carolyn Miller

O mio babbino caro | **GIACOMO PUCCINI**, arr. Carolyn Miller

Piano Trio in G Minor | **CLARA SCHUMANN**, arr. Melody Bober

Symphonie Concertante No. 1 | **CHEVALIER de SAINT-GEORGES**, arr. Eric Baumgartner

Vocalise | **SERGEI RACHMANINOFF**, arr. Eric Baumgartner

William Tell Overture | **GIOACHINO ROSSINI**, arr. Glenda Austin